The Life of Jesus

A Play & Learn Book

Edited by Jill C. Lafferty
Illustrations by Peter Grosshauser

SPARK
HOUSE
FAMILY

Life of Jesus

What if you met someone amazing, someone who talked and acted like no one else you'd ever known? You'd tell all your friends about this person, wouldn't you?

The people who met Jesus, who talked with him and walked with him and loved him, were excited to tell their friends about him too. Their stories about Jesus make up four whole books in the Bible. They are called the Gospels and they have taught us about Jesus for thousands of years.

This Play and Learn book is filled with stories from the Gospels. Four guys named Matthew, Mark, Luke, and John knew all about Jesus and picked the stories that would help others see that Jesus wasn't just an ordinary man, he was the Son of God! So they wrote about Jesus' message of love and kindness and forgiveness. They wrote about Jesus healing people who were sick and caring for people others had forgotten. They wrote about Jesus our friend and Savior.

As you and your family explore your Play and Learn book about the life of Jesus, see if you can find a story where Jesus:

- Talks about loving other people
- Shows kindness to a person others might ignore
- Teaches his friends how to follow God

Each story in this Play and Learn book gives you a verse to remember, some fun activities to try, and ideas for living the way Jesus taught us to. So jump in and discover more about the life of Jesus!

Published by Sparkhouse Family
510 Marquette Avenue
Minneapolis, MN 55402
sparkhouse.org

© 2016 Sparkhouse Family

All rights reserved.

The Life of Jesus Play and Learn Book
First edition published 2016

Printed in United States
21 20 19 18 17 16   1 2 3 4 5 6 7 8
9781506417646

Edited by Jill C. Lafferty
Cover design by Tory Herman
Cover illustration by Peter Grosshauser
Interior designed by Tory Herman
Interior photographs provided by
iStock and Thinkstock
Illustrations by Peter Grosshauser

All Bible quotations are from THE HOLY BIBLE, NEW INTERNATIONAL VERSION®, NIV®. Copyright © 1973, 1978, 1984, 2011 by Biblica, Inc.® Used by permission of Zondervan. All rights reserved worldwide. www.zondervan.com The "NIV" and "New International Version" are trademarks registered in the United States Patent and Trademark Office by Biblica, Inc.™

V63474; 9781506417646; JUN2016

Table of Contents

How to Use Your Spark Story Bible Play and Learn Book

Each section in this Play and Learn book includes a short story from the Bible, followed by all kinds of engaging ways to think about the theme of the story. Look for these activities in every story.

Conversation Starters
Talk about these questions as a family. Make sure everyone gets a chance to share their thoughts.

The Story
Start here. You'll get a summary of the Bible story you'll explore on the pages to come.

A Prayer to Share
Cut out these prayers to help you talk to God about what you've learned.

Explore with Squiggles
This expressive little caterpillar responds to each story with a specific emotion and invites children to do the same.

A blessing is a special welcome from God.

Jesus blessed the children and told them, "God loves you!" Jesus loves children all around the world—including you. Draw yourself, siblings, and friends into the pictures of kids with Jesus.

Draw and Discover
Each story includes simple coloring or drawing activities children can do on their own or with the family.

Do You Know?
The Bible has lots of stories about children. Unscramble these letters to find the names of children in the Bible.

1. E O P S J H
(See Genesis 37:3-28.)

2. A I M I M R
(See Exodus 2:1-10 and Numbers 26:59.)

3. V D I A D
(See 1 Samuel 17:4-11, 32-50.)

A Puzzle to Solve
Word games, mazes, connect-the-dots, and other puzzles and games help you explore the themes of the story.

A Verse to Learn
Say these verses together or try to memorize them as a family.

In the Bible AND In Our World!

School for children in Jesus' time was different. Jewish boys like Jesus were taught reading and writing by rabbis (teachers) in synagogues (places of worship), starting around age 5. At age 10, boys started learning Jewish law. Girls were taught at home by their mothers. Today, boys and girls go to school in most places around the world and learn many different things.

"Let the little children come to me, and do not hinder them,

for the kingdom of God belongs to such as these."
Mark 10:14

There's MORE to this story!
Read the WHOLE story in your Bible together! You can find it in the 2nd book in the New Testament.
Mark 10:13-16
In the Spark Story Bible, look for Jesus Blesses the Children on p.

Look It Up!
Read the whole story for yourselves from your Bible or *Spark Story Bible*.

In Our World
Find out more about how the themes of the stories show up in our lives today.

Make Time for Welcoming Fun!
Jesus welcomed children by telling them, **"You are part of God's family."** The next time you have family friends over, greet them at the door. Smile and say, **"God loves you!"** just like Jesus did.

Family Fun!
Put your learning into action with these family activity ideas.

Jesus' Baptism

Jesus changes us.

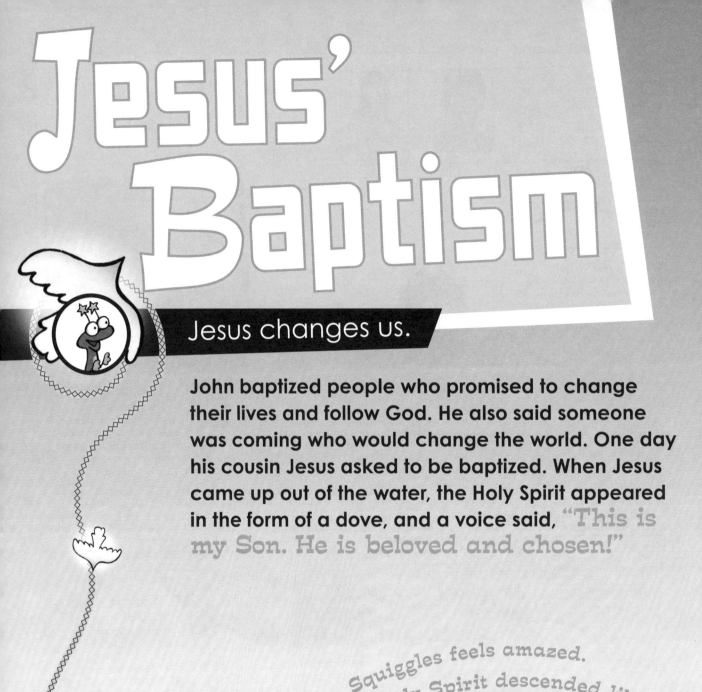

John baptized people who promised to change their lives and follow God. He also said someone was coming who would change the world. One day his cousin Jesus asked to be baptized. When Jesus came up out of the water, the Holy Spirit appeared in the form of a dove, and a voice said, "This is my Son. He is beloved and chosen!"

Squiggles feels amazed.
The Holy Spirit descended like a dove!

How does YOUR face look when you feel amazed?

Cut out this prayer and tape it near your bathtub or shower. Say the prayer before bath time, then watch your skin change from dirty to clean!

GOD, thank you for sending Jesus and marking him and us with your love. Amen.

WHAT ABOUT YOU HAS CHANGED RECENTLY?

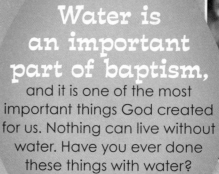

Water is an important part of baptism,

and it is one of the most important things God created for us. Nothing can live without water. Have you ever done these things with water?

Draw your favorite thing to do with water.

Make Time for Interview Fun!

John baptized Jesus in a river. He may have gone all the way under water! Think of someone in your family who has been baptized and interview them about their experience. Remember the WHO, WHAT, WHEN, WHERE, WHY, and HOW questions of an interview:

WHO participated in their baptism?

WHAT does their baptism mean to them?

WHEN were they baptized?

WHERE were they baptized?

WHY did they get baptized?

HOW were they baptized?

In the Bible AND In Our World!

John baptized Jesus at the Jordan River. Today, the Jordan River flows 156 miles, through the Sea of Galilee, ending in the Dead Sea.

Sea of Galilee

L.Tiberias (Sea of Galilee)

Nazareth

Jordan River

Jerusalem

Jericho

Bethlehem

Dead Sea

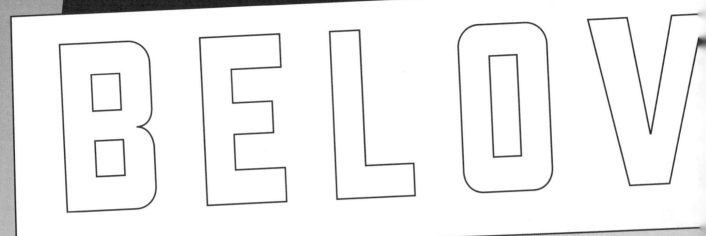

BELOV

COLOR THIS WORD. The word *beloved* goes beyond meaning that a person is loved. It means that a person is cherished, precious, priceless, and loved in more ways than can be counted. Jesus is beloved by God. *You are beloved by God!*

Do You Know?

Matthew 28:16-20 is a famous Bible passage known as the GREAT COMMISSION. In these verses, Jesus tells his disciples to make more people disciples and to baptize everyone in the name of the

_____, the

_____, and the

_____ _____ .

[Hint: See Matthew 28:19.]

And a voice from heaven said

"This is my Son, whom I love

Make Time for Water Fun!

Take time as a family to go on a walk near a body of water close to your home—an ocean, a lake, a river, a stream, a pond, or even a mud puddle. **What lives in and around the water?** Why is this water important? **How does this water and this place change with the seasons?**

with him I am well pleased."

Matthew 3:17

Gather together and read this verse out oud, naming each amily member in the place of "my Son." A reader could go o another room and oudly read the verse, o that only the voice s heard. Then each erson named may uess from which room he voice is coming.

There's MORE to this story!

Read the WHOLE story in your Bible together! You can find it in the first 3 books in the New Testament:

Matthew 3:13-17; Mark 1:4-11; and Luke 3:15-17, 21-22

In the Spark Story Bible, look for Jesus' Baptism on pages 224–227.

11

The Disciples

We are disciples too!

FOLLOW ME.... FOLLOW ME.... FOLLOW ME.... FOLLOW ME.... FOLLOW ME.... FOLLOW ME.... FOLLOW ME.... FOLLOW ME.... FOLLOW ME.... FOLLOW ME....

Jesus called men and women to help build God's kingdom. He asked fishermen to catch people instead of fish. He asked tax collectors to collect people instead of money. Lots of different people stopped doing what they were doing and started helping Jesus spread God's word.

A disciple is someone who follows the teachings of another person.

Squiggles feels proud to follow Jesus.

How does YOUR face look when you feel proud?

FOLLOW ME.... FOLLOW ME.... FOLLOW ME....

Cut out this prayer and tape it to your front door. Say it together every time you leave your home.

JESUS, we want to be your disciples and spread your word in the world! Amen.

HOW DO YOU FOLLOW JESUS? WHAT WOULD BE HARD TO GIVE UP FOR JESUS?

FOLLOW ME. . . . FOLLOW ME. . . . FOLLOW ME. . . . FOLLOW ME. . . . FOLLOW ME. . . . FOLLOW

Here is some pronunciation help:
Zebedee is pronounced ZEH-beh-dee.
Bartholomew is pronounced bar-THAHL-uh-my
Alphaeus is pronounced AL-fee-uhs.
Thaddaeus is pronounced THAD-dee-uhs.
Zealot is pronounced ZEL-ot.
Iscariot is pronounced iss-CARE-ree-ut.

These are the names of the twelve apostles:
first, Simon, who is called Peter,
and his brother Andrew;
James son of Zebedee,
and his brother John;
Philip and Bartholomew;
Thomas and Matthew the tax collector;
James son of Alphaeus,
and Thaddaeus;
Simon the Zealot,
and Judas Iscariot, who betrayed him.

Matthew 10:2-4

Have you ever tried to memorize the names of the 12 disciples?

Work together with family or friends to make up a song with all of the disciples' names. Use a familiar tune such as "Twinkle, Twinkle Little Star." After you learn it, teach it to someone else!

FOLLOW ME. . . . FOLLOW ME. . . . FOLLOW ME. . . . FOLLOW ME. . . . FOLLOW ME. . . . FOLLOW ME. . .

People from lots of different backgrounds became Jesus' disciples.

People who follow Jesus today have lots of different jobs too. Look at the photos. How do you think these people follow Jesus while doing their job?

Put a ☆ by a job that the disciples had. Put a ☺ on jobs that you might like to do when you grow up.

Make Time for Fishing Fun!

Go "fishing" like some of the disciples. Lay out a blue blanket, get a large box or tub for a boat and tie a string to a pole or stick. In the boat talk about fishing for fish and "fishing" for people.

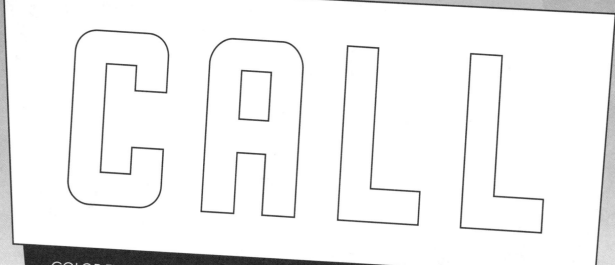

COLOR THIS WORD. When God "calls" people, God invites them to do something. God called the disciples to follow Jesus and share God's word. We are all called to follow God, but we serve God in different ways.

Make Time for Fish Eating Fun!

Plan a fish fry for family and friends. If you don't have a favorite family recipe for fish, go online with an adult to find one to try. Work together to make the meal. While you eat the fish dinner, talk about all the different ways to follow Jesus.

FOLLOW ME. . . . FOLLOW ME. . . . FOLLOW ME. . . . FOLLOW ME. . . . FOLLOW ME. . . . FOLLOW ME. . . .

In the Bible AND In Our World!

Jesus started with **12** disciples and other men and woman who followed him.

Today there are **2.18 BILLION DISCIPLES** in the world! That's **2,180,000,000** people!

NEARLY 1/3 of the people on earth describe themselves as Christian, or followers of Jesus. That number has **QUADRUPLED** in the last **100 YEARS**.

There is no one country that is the "center" of Christianity. You'll find Christians almost everywhere you go!

There's MORE to this story!

Read the WHOLE story in your Bible together!
You can find it in 2 Gospel books:

Matthew 4:12-23, 9:9-13, 10:1-4;
Luke 5:1-11, 8:1-3

In the Spark Story Bible, look for
The Disciples on pages 232–237.

Wedding at Cana

Let's celebrate Jesus!

Jesus was with his friends at a wedding party. Suddenly the wine ran out! Jesus' mother, Mary, asked Jesus to help. Jesus took six large clay jars of water and turned the water into wine. The party could go on! This was Jesus' first miracle, and everyone was amazed. **Jesus' friends knew he was God's Son.**

Squiggles feels worried. Can Jesus help the party?

How does YOUR face look when you feel worried?

Cut out this prayer and tape it to a party hat or another hat you have. Take turns wearing the hat and saying the prayer. End with a celebration cheer!

GOD, thank you for all the wonderful things we have to celebrate together! Amen.

WHAT DO YOU LIKE ABOUT CELEBRATIONS?
HOW DO YOU CELEBRATE?

Jesus and his friends were celebrating at a wedding

when Jesus turned water into wine. What special events do you celebrate? Color the balloons on the photos of events that you have celebrated.

Make Time for Water Fun!

Jesus turned water into wine. You can do some fun things to change water too. Have an adult help you pour water into a few glasses or clear cups. Add a few drops of food coloring to one or more of the glasses and watch the water turn colors. Add some lemon, lime, or orange juice or crushed fresh mint to other glasses and taste the difference.

Which is your favorite?

What Jesus did here in Cana of Galilee was the first of the signs through which he revealed his glory; and his disciples believed in him.
John 2:11

Jesus' miracles are amazing things to celebrate. Gather party hats, noisemakers, and streamers. Stand in a circle and read this Bible verse together. Then celebrate Jesus with lots of noise and movement!

Make Time for Party Fun!

We can celebrate Jesus any time. Invite friends over for a party like the one in this story. Serve grape juice and tell your friends the story of Jesus' miracle. Then dance to music and praise God!

In the Bible AND In Our World!

In Jesus' time, a large clay jar for storing wine or water was called an amphora. These are the kind of jars in this story. Today, the water and other drinks we consume may be stored in glass or plastic bottles or cartons.

Amphora is pronounced **AM-for-uh.**

Do You Know?

The Bible has several stories about celebrating. Who partied (and praised God) in these stories?

1. _____ sang a song and women danced after the Israelites safely crossed the Red Sea. *(See Exodus 15:20-21.)*

2. A _____ threw a party when his prodigal son returned home. *(See Luke 15:22-24.)*

3. A _____ gave a wedding banquet for his son. When the invited guests didn't come, he sent his servants to invite people off the streets. *(See Matthew 22:2-3, 8-10.)*

There's MORE to this story!

Read the WHOLE story in your Bible together! You can find it in the 4th book in the New Testament:

John 2:1-11

In the Spark Story Bible, look for Wedding at Cana on pages 332–337.

Jesus Heals

We believe God heals.

One of the most amazing things about Jesus is that he healed people. When Simon's mother-in-law had a fever, Jesus healed her. The news about his miracles spread quickly! People came to see him, hoping to be healed. Jesus' disciples knew that people needed to see Jesus!

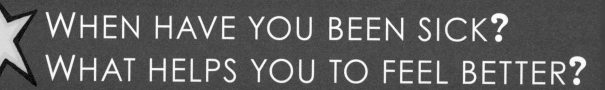

WHEN HAVE YOU BEEN SICK?
WHAT HELPS YOU TO FEEL BETTER?

Cut out this prayer and tape it to the door of your medicine cabinet. Say the prayer together whenever an adult gets medicine for someone in your family.

GOD, thank you for healing our bodies, inside and out. Amen.

Squiggles feels amazed! Jesus healed a woman with a fever.

How does YOUR face look when you feel amazed?

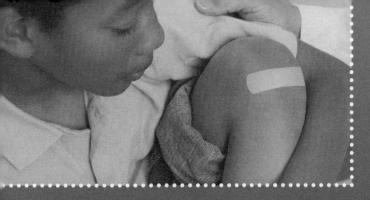

All people need healing sometimes.

Look at the photos together. Color in the ♡ on the photos that show things that have happened to you. Who helped you heal?

Make Time for More Fun!

Take time to learn about how to help heal minor injuries at home. Look online with an adult to learn about basic first aid. Pretend to have an injury, and practice the proper way to clean, treat, and cover a minor scrape or cut.

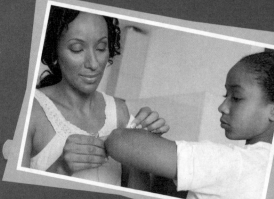

Very early in the morning, while it was still dark, Jesus got up, left the house and went off to a solitary place, where he prayed.

Mark 1:35

Some sicknesses, injuries, and conditions don't get better. But we can always pray for people. Say this verse together, and pray for everyone you know who needs healing.

In the Bible AND In Our World!

When people in Bible times suffered from diseases, they were outcast—they were separated from the community. When Jesus healed people, he made them well and brought them back into the community. Many of the diseases of Bible times are easily cured today with modern medicine. But people still get sick and need healing! Medicine helps when we are sick, but we also need the love and support of those around us.

There's MORE to this story!

Read the WHOLE story in your Bible together! You can find it in the 2nd book of the New Testament:

Mark 1:29-39

In the Spark Story Bible, look for Jesus Heals on pages 230–231.

Woman at the Well

We're thirsty, Lord!

After a long walk in a place called Samaria, Jesus stopped to rest at a well. A Samaritan woman saw him and gave him a drink of water from the well. Jesus offered her a different kind of water. He called it "living water." The woman realized that Jesus was the Messiah, the anointed one, and ran to tell everyone.

Squiggles feels thirsty.

He wants living water too! How does YOUR face look when you feel thirsty?

Cut out this prayer. Use crayons or markers to color the jug, "filling" it with water as you say the prayer.

DEAR JESUS, thank you for filling us up with your living water of love, forgiveness, and new life! Amen.

WHAT'S YOUR FAVORITE DRINK WHEN YOU ARE THIRSTY? WHY?

Where do people around the world get their drinking water?

Where do you get yours?

Draw a cross on each picture to remember Jesus offers living water to everyone!

There's MORE to this story!

Read the WHOLE story in your Bible together! You can find it in the New Testament, in the 4th Gospel:

John 4:5-42

In the Spark Story Bible, look for Woman at the Well on pages 338–343.

Mediterranean Sea
LEBANON
SYRIA
IRAQ
Sea of Galilee
Nablus
Jerusalem
Bethlehem
Dead Sea
ISRAEL
EGYPT
JORDAN
SAUDI ARABIA
Gulf of Aqaba

In the Bible AND In Our World!

The place where Jesus stopped for water was near a town called Samaria. Samaria was located in what today is near the town of Nablus in Jordan. The well is called, "Jacob's well." You can still visit Jacob's well today—nearly 2,000 years later! A church, the Bir Ya'qub Monastery, has been built around it.

Jesus answered, "Everyone who drinks this water will be thirsty again, but whoever drinks the water I give them will never thirst. Indeed, the water I give them will become in them a spring of water welling up to eternal life."
John 4:13-14

Make Time for More Fun!

Samaritans were outcasts in Jesus' time. Many Jewish people didn't want to be near them. Jesus reached out to the Samaritan woman anyway. How can your family show kindness to someone who might feel left out in your church or community?

Can you visit an elderly person?
Volunteer to serve at a soup kitchen?
Smile at everyone you see today?

Fill a glass with water. Read these Bible verses out loud. Take a sip of water any time you hear the words *drink*, *water*, or *thirsty*. How many sips did you take? Give everyone a turn to sip and count!

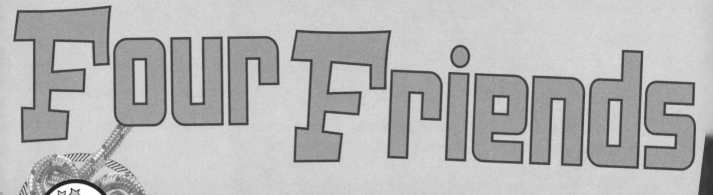

Four Friends

Let's take care of our friends.

Four friends had a friend who couldn't walk. They knew Jesus could help their friend, but Jesus was in a house crowded with people, and they couldn't get their friend in. The man's friends carried him to the roof and used ropes to lower him into the room. Jesus forgave the man's sins and healed him!

★ HOW CAN YOU HELP FRIENDS?

HOW DO FRIENDS HELP YOU?

Cut out this prayer, punch holes in the corners, and write names of friends on the other side of the card. Tie string or ribbon to each corner. With friends and family, raise this prayer by the strings as you say it together.

Squiggles feels shocked. A man is coming through the roof.

How does **YOUR** face look when you feel shocked?

GOD, we lift our friends up to you in prayer. Amen.

The man who couldn't walk was carried by his friends so that he could see Jesus.

Why do you think people are being carried in these photos? Who carries you? Who do you carry?

Draw a picture of a time when you were carried by someone.

There's MORE to this story.

Read the WHOLE story in your Bible together! You can find it in the 3rd book in the New Testament

Luke 5:17-26

In the Spark Story Bible, look for *Four Friends* on pages 288–293.

Do You Know?

Four friends in this story helped their friend who couldn't walk. Here are some other Bible BFFs—but their names are scrambled! Can you unscramble the names of these friends? If you get stuck, look up the verses for a clue.

1. OAMIN & THUR *(See Ruth 1:16-18.)*

_ _ _ _ _ & _ _ _ _

2. VIDAD & THOJANAN *(See 1 Samuel 18:3.)*

_ _ _ _ _ &

_ _ _ _ _ _ _ _ _

3. LUAP & LISSA *(Acts 16:25.)*

_ _ _ _ & _ _ _ _ _

Friend, your sins are forgiven. Luke 5:20

When Jesus forgave the man's sins, he was saying that God let go of the things that the man had done that hurt God and other people.

What words can you use to ask for forgiveness when you hurt a friend? Write them here.

What words can you use to forgive a friend? Write them here.

Make Time for More Fun!

Find a friend about your size and work together to lift each other up. Sit on the ground back to back. Link your arms together, and then stand up by pushing against each other. How hard is it to lift each other up? **How hard would it have been for the four friends to carry the man to Jesus?**

Do You Know? Answers: 1. Naomi & Ruth; 2. David & Jonathan; 3. Paul & Silas

35

The Beatitudes

Jesus blesses us.

One day Jesus climbed a mountain and told a crowd about the people God blesses: people who feel hopeless, sad, and hurt; people who don't have a lot of things; people who want to follow God; kind people; people who know what is right in their heart; and people who make peace. This wasn't what people expected to hear! Jesus' message about who God blesses is called *the Beatitudes.*

Squiggles feels blessed. God cares about him!

How does YOUR face look when you feel blessed?

WHO IS A BLESSING TO YOUR FAMILY?

HOW DO YOU FEEL BLESSED?

To be **blessed by God** means that God looks upon you with favor.

Cut out this prayer and tape it to a mirror that the family uses. Every time you comb your hair, say this prayer.

BLESS ME, God, so I may be a blessing to others. Amen.

Jesus told the crowd about people who God blesses.

Draw a line from the photo to the word that describes the person in the photo.

God blesses:

People who are **KIND**

People who are **HOPELESS**

The **PEACEMAKERS**

People who are **PERSECUTED** (treated badly by others) in my name

People who **MOURN** (sad because someone died)

There's **MORE** to this story!

Read the WHOLE story in your Bible together! You can find it in the 1st book of the New Testament:

Matthew 5:1-12

In the Spark Story Bible, look for *The Beatitudes* on pages 238–241.

the earth; 2. enemies; 3. judge

RESTORES MY SOUL. HE RESTORES MY SOUL. HE RESTORES MY SOUL. HE REST

Blessed are the peacemakers, for they will be called children of God.
Matthew 5:9

Jesus says that people who make peace will be blessed. **What does it mean to be a peacemaker?** The answer can be different for each person. Talk about how each member of your family can be a peacemaker in their own unique way.

1. When are things not peaceful in our family?

2. How can we be peacemakers in those situations?

Make Time for More Fun!

Does your family know someone who is sad, feels hopeless, or is hungry? Maybe your family knows a person who needs prayers and other help. Talk about how you could help this person and show that he or she is blessed by God. Put your words into action, and come up with a specific plan to help.

Do You Know?

The Beatitudes were just the beginning of a long sermon Jesus told the crowd on the mountain. What other things did Jesus teach on that important day? Use your Bible to discover the surprising things Jesus said.

3. "Do not
_____."
(See Matthew 7:1.)

2. "Love your
_____."
(See Matthew 5:44.)

1. "You are the
_____."
(See Matthew 5:13.)

Do Not Worry

God takes care of us!

Jesus wanted the people he taught to know that they didn't need to worry about things. God feeds the birds and God will feed you, Jesus explained. God makes the flowers colorful, and God makes you beautiful too. Don't worry. God takes care of us!

WHO TAKES CARE OF YOU?
WHO CAN YOU TRUST?

Cut out this prayer and tape it to your refrigerator. Say it whenever you get a snack.

GOD, thanks for taking care of us so we don't have to worry. Amen.

Squiggles feels happy. God takes care of him!

How does YOUR face look when you feel happy?

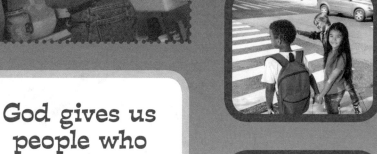

God gives us people who take care of us.

Look at the photos. The people in the photos with the blue border need help. The people in the photos with the yellow border are helpers. Match the people who need help with the person who will help them.

There's MORE to this story!

Read the WHOLE story in your Bible together! You can find it in the 1st Gospel book:

Matthew 6:24-34

In the Spark Story Bible, look for the New Testament story titled *Do Not Worry* on pages 244–245.

Therefore do not worry about tomorrow, for tomorrow will worry about itself. Each day has enough trouble of its own.

Matthew 6:34

Write this verse on a piece of paper and tape it above a toilet in your home. Using a marker, write down something you worry about on toilet paper. Flush your worries, while saying the verse together with family members. We don't have to worry because God takes care of us!

Make Time for More Fun!

Go to a local flower shop or take a walk outside. What kinds of flowers do you see? How many colors and patterns do you find? God created each flower in unique and beautiful colors, and God makes you unique and beautiful too!

In the Bible AND In Our World!

Jesus told the people not to worry about what they will wear. In Bible times, both men and women wore long, loose-fitting garments, often made of wool or linen, and sandals. Bible stories happened in the Middle East, where it is often hot and dry. Loose-fitting clothing helped people feel cool.

Love Your Enemies

God helps us love everyone.

When Jesus taught people about God, he shared some surprising news: When someone hurts you, don't hurt them back. Help everyone. Share what you have with other people. And Jesus told people that they should love everyone—friends AND enemies. That really shook people up!

WHEN IS IT EASY TO LOVE SOMEONE?

WHEN IS IT HARD TO LOVE SOMEONE?

LOVING GOD, help us to love everyone we meet the way you love all of us. Amen.

Cut out this prayer and tape it to the front door of your home. Say the prayer every time you leave the house.

Squiggles feels surprised by Jesus' words.

How does YOUR face look when you feel surprised?

E OF MY   YOU PREPARE A TABL   RESENCE OF MY ENE   REP

There are times when it's easy to love, and times when it is hard to love.

Look at the photos. Color the hearts red if the photo shows a situation where it is "easy" to love. What words could be used in the "hard to love" photos to change the situation?

Make Time for More Fun!

How many different ways do you know to say the word *love*? Here are the words for *love* in the five most spoken languages in the world today:

Mandarin = ài (EYE)

Spanish = amor (ah-MORE)

English = love

Hindi = pyaar (pea-ARH)

Arabic = hubb

With an adult, use the Internet to search for the word *love* in even more languages.

American Sign Language for "love"

ORE ME

MY ENEM

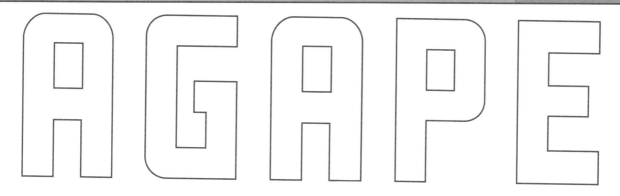

AGAPE

COLOR THIS WORD. Agape is a Greek word that means "love"—especially God's love for us and the sharing of God's love with others. When we love our "enemies" as well as our friends, we experience agape love.

Agape is pronounced **ah-GAH-pay**.

You have heard that it was said, "Love your neighbor

(cross your arms over yourself as if you were giving yourself a hug)

and hate your enemy."

(hold hands out with thumbs down)

But I tell you, love your enemies

(turn thumbs up)

and pray for those who persecute you.

(hold hands in prayer)

Matthew 5:43-44

To **persecute** someone is to treat the person badly.

Sit in a circle and say the verse together several times with the actions. Talk about ways you can respond when someone treats you badly.

There's MORE to this story!

Read the WHOLE story in your Bible together! You can find it in the 1st book of the New Testament.

Matthew 5:38-48

In the Spark Story Bible, look for Love Your Enemies on pages 242–243.

... YOU PREPARE A TABLE BEFORE ME IN THE PRESENCE OF MY ENEMIES ...

The Lord's Prayer

We can talk with God.

Jesus' disciples wanted to learn how to pray. "Teach us," they said to Jesus. Jesus said that prayer is a time to think only about God and that using loud voices and big words isn't important. Then Jesus gave the disciples a prayer. We call it "The Lord's Prayer" and we still pray it today.

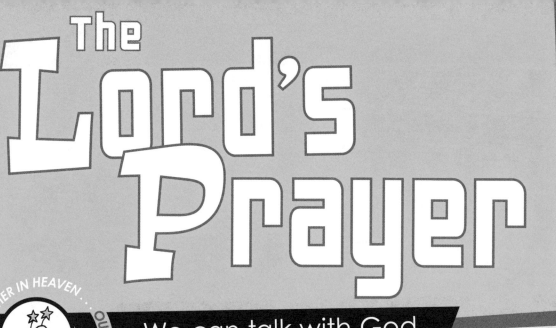

Squiggles feels eager. He wants to learn more about prayer.

How does YOUR face look when you feel eager?

Cut out this prayer and put it next to a family member's bed. Pray the prayer together when you go to sleep and when you wake up.

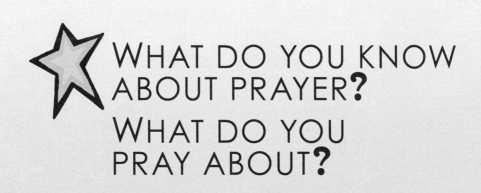

DEAR GOD, praying helps us grow close to you. Thank you for always listening. Amen.

★ WHAT DO YOU KNOW ABOUT PRAYER? WHAT DO YOU PRAY ABOUT?

Do you pray standing up, sitting, or kneeling?

What do you do with your hands?

Do you close your eyes or keep them open

Put a ✓ by the pictures that show how you sometimes look when you are praying.

Make Time for Journal Fun!

Keep a prayer journal by yourself or as a family. Think of it as writing a letter to God or drawing a picture for God. You can share all of your feelings with God: happy, sad, angry, confused, curious. **God will always listen.**

Do You Know?

The Bible records two versions of the Lord's Prayer, one in Matthew and one in Luke.
Read and compare the two. Draw a line under some words that are the same.
Draw a circle around some words that are different. Which prayer do you like better?

MATTHEW 6:9-13

Our Father in heaven,

hallowed be your name,

your kingdom come,

your will be done,
on earth as it is in heaven.

Give us today our daily bread.

And forgive us our debts,

as we also have forgiven
our debtors.

And lead us not
into temptation,

but deliver us from the evil one.

LUKE 11:2-4

Father,

hallowed be your name,

your kingdom come.

Give us each day our daily bread.

Forgive us our sins,

for we also forgive everyone who
sins against us.

And lead us not
into temptation.

In the Bible AND In Our World!

Jesus taught his disciples to pray the Lord's Prayer. Christians all over the world still say the prayer today, but they don't say it in the same way. Survey people you know about the Lord's Prayer. How many different answers do you get to these questions?

Question	Interview 1	Interview 2	Interview 3
Who are you?			
How old were you when you learned the Lord's Prayer?			
What language do you pray it in?			
Where do you pray it?			
When do you pray it?			
Who do you pray it with?			

THER IN

There's MORE to this story!

Read the WHOLE story in your Bible together! You can find it in the 1st book in the New Testament:

Matthew 6:5-15

In the Spark Story Bible, look for The Lord's Prayer on pages 246–249.

This, then, is how you should pray:

Our Father in heaven,

hallowed be your name.

Matthew 6:9

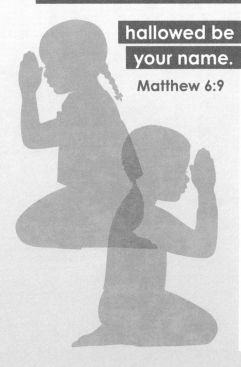

Go to a place in your home together where you like to pray and say the words of this verse. Add your own prayer after the verse.

Then go to a place in your home where another family member likes to pray, repeat the verse and add a prayer.

Find a place for each family member.

Make Time for Singing Fun!

One way to pray is to sing the words! Try singing this prayer to the tune of "London Bridge." After singing the last line, one person says a short prayer. Repeat so that each person has a turn offering a prayer.

God is listening when we pray,

Every night, every day.

God is listening when we pray,

What will we say?

... OUR FATHER IN HEAVEN ... OUR FATHER IN HEAVEN ... OUR FATHER IN HEAVEN ... OUR FATHER IN HEAVEN ... OUR FATHER IN HEAVEN

53

Jesus Feeds 5,000

We can help Jesus.

A crowd came to hear Jesus. Jesus and the disciples knew the moms, dads, and kids were hungry. What would Jesus do? A boy offered 2 fish and 5 loaves of bread. Jesus blessed and shared the food with 5,000 people. *It was a miracle!*

WHAT IS IT LIKE TO BE HUNGRY? WHAT HAVE YOU SHARED?

Squiggles feels amazed. There's enough for everyone!

How does **YOUR** face look when you feel amazed?

Cut out this prayer and post it on your refrigerator. Say it together as you make a meal.

DEAR JESUS, Thanks for feeding us. Help us to share what we have. Amen.

A boy helped Jesus share what the people needed.

You have things to share too!

Draw a ♥ on the photos of things you can share, and write 1 thing you can share on the line.

Jesus then took the loaves, gave thanks, and distributed to those who were seated as much as they wanted. He did the same with the fish.

John 6:11

Make a "fish sandwich" while reading this verse:

Sit on a couch with your family. Adults sit in the middle—they are the fish! Kids sit on the edges—they are the bread! As the "fish" read the verse, the "bread" hugs the "fish."

There's MORE to this story!

Read the WHOLE story in your Bible together! You can find it in the 4th Gospel book:

John 6:1-14

In the Spark Story Bible, look for Jesus Feeds 5,000 on pages 344–349.

Make Time for Baking Fun!

Sharing a meal is a wonderful way to show love and care for others. As a family, bake a loaf of homemade bread, then invite friends to your house to share it with you.

Do You Know?

Are you hungry? Many different foods are mentioned in the Bible. Look up these Bible verses. Make a healthy "meal" with the foods you discover by drawing them on the plate.

1. Song of Solomon 2:5

2. Matthew 6:11

3. John 21:6

Add one of your favorite foods to the plate too.

58

What does this word mean to you?

MIRACLE

COLOR THIS WORD. A *miracle* is an amazing event that can't be explained. The Bible includes many stories of Jesus performing miracles: healing people who were sick, raising the dead, and feeding thousands of people with small amounts of food.

Make Time for Penny Fun!

Jesus fed thousands of people with a tiny amount of food shared by one boy. Sometimes little things make a big difference. Search your home for loose change. Place the coins you find in a jar and add a label that says: "We Care! We Share!" Add more each day. When the jar is full, donate the money to a cause your family cares about.

Jesus Blesses the Children

Welcome to God's family!

One day Jesus was speaking to a large crowd. Everyone wanted to see Jesus. Some children moved in closer. Jesus' disciples tried to shoo the children away. "Wait!" Jesus said. "I want the children to sit by me." Jesus smiled at the children and said, *"Welcome to God's family!"*

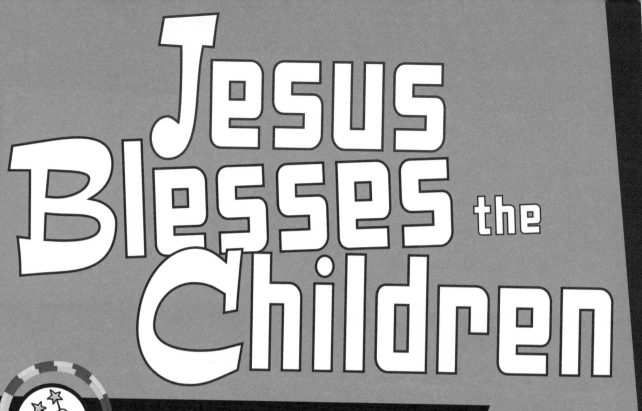

Squiggles feels welcomed by Jesus. He's a part of God's family.

How does YOUR face look when you feel welcomed?

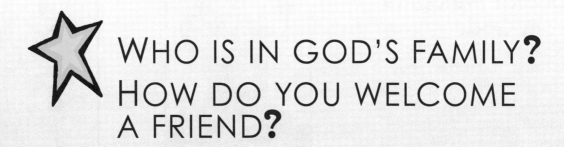

WHO IS IN GOD'S FAMILY?
HOW DO YOU WELCOME A FRIEND?

Cut out this prayer and tape it to your front door. Stand near the door and pray the prayer together.

**DEAR GOD,
Help us to welcome people who come to our home. Amen.**

A blessing is a special welcome from God.

Jesus blessed the children and told them, "God loves you!" Jesus loves children all around the world—including you. Draw yourself, siblings, and friends into the pictures of kids with Jesus.

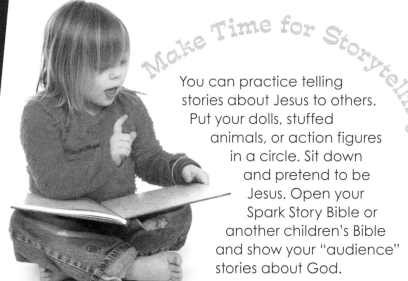

Make Time for Storytelling Fun!

You can practice telling stories about Jesus to others. Put your dolls, stuffed animals, or action figures in a circle. Sit down and pretend to be Jesus. Open your Spark Story Bible or another children's Bible and show your "audience" stories about God.

Do You Know?

The Bible has lots of stories about children. Unscramble these letters to find the names of children in the Bible.

1. EOPSJH
(See Genesis 37:1-28.)

____ ____ ____ ____ ____ ____

2. AIMIMR
(See Exodus 2:1-10 and Numbers 26:59.)

____ ____ ____ ____ ____ ____

3. VDIAD
(See 1 Samuel 17:4-11, 32-50.)

____ ____ ____ ____ ____

4. HAMIEERJ
(See Jeremiah 1:4-10.)

____ ____ ____ ____ ____ ____ ____ ____

Do You Know? Answers
1. Joseph, 2. Miriam,
3. David, 4. Jeremiah.

In the Bible AND In Our World!

School for children in Jesus' time was different. Jewish boys like Jesus were taught reading and writing by rabbis (teachers) in synagogues (places of worship), starting around age 5. At age 10, boys started learning Jewish law. Girls were taught at home by their mothers. Today, boys and girls go to school in most places around the world, and learn many different subjects.

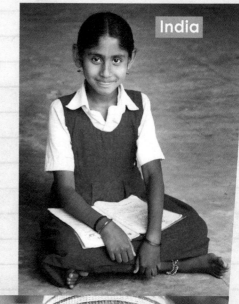
India

Africa

Middle East

North America

Israel

When Jesus saw this, he was indignant. He said to them,

"Let the little children come to me, and do not hinder them,

for the kingdom of God belongs to such as these."
Mark 10:14

There's MORE to this story!
Read the WHOLE story in your Bible together! You can find it in the 2nd book in the New Testament:

Mark 10:13-16

In the Spark Story Bible, look for Jesus Blesses the Children on pages 272–277.

Play a game to remember this verse. Use toys or blocks to create an obstacle course leading to a Bible.

Step over or walk around the toys as you repeat the words, "Let the little children come to me, and do not hinder them."

Make Time for Welcoming Fun!

Jesus welcomed children by telling them, **"You are part of God's family."** The next time you have family friends over, greet them at the door. Smile and say, **"God loves you!"** just like Jesus did.

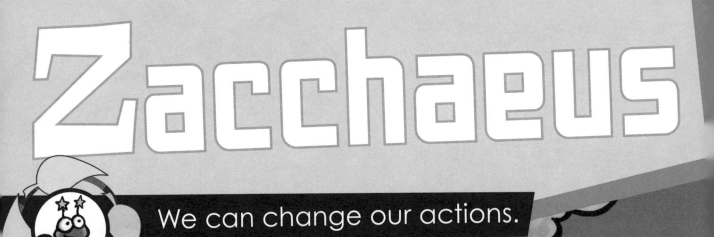

Zacchaeus

We can change our actions.

Zacchaeus was a tax collector who lived in Jericho. People hated Zacchaeus because he took their money. Jesus went to Zacchaeus's house for dinner and told him that God wants us to love each other.

Zacchaeus listened, changed his ways, and returned the money he took.

Squiggles feels eager to follow Jesus.

How does YOUR face look when you feel eager to do the right thing?

WHY DO WE SOMETIMES HATE OTHERS?

HOW CAN WE LOVE INSTEAD?

Cut out this prayer and hang it from a string in a place where you gather. Pray it together when you need to make better choices.

DEAR JESUS, sometimes we make bad choices. Like Zacchaeus, we know that you can help us change. Amen.

Jesus told Zacchaeus about God's love.

Talk about the feelings in each picture. How can love change the situation? Put a star next to pictures that show feelings you have had today.

Make Time for Outdoor Fun!

Zacchaeus climbed a tree to see Jesus. Climbing trees is fun, but finding a good climbing tree can be hard. Go on a family walk. Look for big trees with low branches. The branches you climb must be as big as the top of your arm. Have an adult help you climb and keep you safe. What do you see?

Do You Know?

Zacchaeus was short, so he climbed a sycamore tree to see Jesus. Unscramble the names of these trees that are found in the Bible. If you get stuck, look up the verse for a clue.

1. koa (Genesis 13:18) ___ ___ ___

2. drace (1 Kings 5:6-7) ___ ___ ___ ___ ___

3. llowwi (Psalm 137:2) ___ ___ ___ ___ ___ ___

4. ccaaai (Isaiah 41:19) ___ ___ ___ ___ ___ ___

5. lamp (John 12:13) ___ ___ ___ ___

Make Time for Family Fun!

Zacchaeus wasn't tall—he was "short of stature." Stand in line as a family from the shortest to the tallest. Use a measuring tape to measure everyone in your family. Mark the heights on a strip of paper. Measure your family each month. Who is changing and getting taller? Who is the same?

> "Zacchaeus, come down immediately. I must stay at your house today." So he came down at once and welcomed him gladly. All the people saw this and began to mutter, "He has gone to be the guest of a sinner."
>
> Luke 19:5-7

Why would the people grumble?

List the reasons the people would grumble about Jesus.

List the reasons you grumble.

There's MORE to this story!
Read the WHOLE story in your Bible together! You can find it near the end of the 3rd Gospel, the book of Luke:

Luke 19:1-10
In the Spark Story Bible, look for Zacchaeus on pages 326–331.

The Greatest

We love each other!

The Pharisees were trying to trick Jesus, so they asked him what God's most important commandment was. How could he pick just one? Jesus said to love God with all your heart, soul, and mind, and love your neighbor as yourself. If you obey these two laws, then you obey all the laws!

Commandment

HOW DO YOU SHOW LOVE TO GOD?
HOW DO YOU SHOW LOVE TO OTHERS?

Squiggles feels scared. The Pharisees are tricky. How does YOUR face look when you feel scared?

Cut out this prayer and tuck it in your pillowcase. Say it together every night this week before you go to sleep.

We love you, God, with all our hearts, all our souls, and all our minds. Help us love everyone! Amen.

LOVE GOD! LOVE OTHERS! LOVE GOD! LOVE OTHERS! HERS!

There are lots of ways to show love to each other.

Look at the photos. Have you ever shown love in these ways? In the heart, draw your favorite way to show love to others.

LOVE GOD! LOVE OTH... ...OTHERS! LOVE O

Make Time for Kindness Fun!

As a family, do something kind to show love to your neighbors. Weed a friend's garden or shovel their driveway. Leave cookies on a neighbor's doorstep. Read a book to a younger neighbor. Visit an older neighbor. What other kind actions can you think of?

Love your neighbor as yourself.
Matthew 22:39

As a family, make a list of ways you can show love to one another. Put Jesus' commandment at the top. Where will you put the list as a reminder to each other?

1. Love God.

2. Love others.

3.

4.

5.

6.

There's MORE to this story!

Read the WHOLE story in your Bible together! You can find it in the 1st Gospel book:

Matthew 22:34-46

In the Spark Story Bible, look for the New Testament story titled The Greatest Commandment on pages 268–271.

LOVE OTHERS! LOVE G

VE OTHERS! LOVE GOD! LOVE OTHERS! LOVE GO

NEIGHB

COLOR THIS WORD. Jesus says we should love our neighbors. Who is your neighbor? Neighbors live next to you, but Jesus also means that we should be kind to anyone we meet!

In the Bible and In Our World

God told the Jewish people to put the shema everywhere: on doorframes, on their hands, even on their foreheads! When the shema is placed on a doorpost, it is called a *mezuzah* (meh-ZOO-zah). When it is worn on a head or arm, it is called a *tefillin* (TEH-fill-in). Where could you put the words of Jesus' greatest commandment as a reminder?

LOVE GOD! LOVE OTHERS! LOVE GOD! LOVE OTHERS! LOVE GOD! LOVE OTHERS! LOVE GOD! LO

Do You Know?

For Jewish people, the Greatest Commandment is called the *shema* (shih-MAH). Read Deuteronomy 6:4-9. What instructions did God give the people about the shema? Use the word bank to fill in the answers.

Word Bank
doorpost
home
lying
home
children
arm

1. Teach it to your _____ .

2. Say it when you're _____ down.

3. Say it when you're at _____

   AND away from _____ .

4. Bind it to your _____ .

5. Write it on your _____

   _____ .

LOVE GOD! LOVE OTHERS! LOVE GOD! LOVE OTHERS! LOVE GOD! LOVE OTHERS! LOVE GOD! LOVE OTHERS!

77

A Note for Grown-Ups

At Sparkhouse Family, we believe faith formation isn't something that only happens when kids are in church or hearing a Bible story in Sunday school. It's an ongoing process that's part of every moment of a child's life. Each interaction with a caring adult shows kids what love looks like. Each playful interaction with a friend taps into their God-given joy and delight. Moments of daydreaming and imaginative play develop their ability to see God in the world.

We also know that many families want to create intentional times of spiritual formation for their kids. That's where the Spark Story Bible Play and Learn books come in. Whether you've already introduced your children to the Bible or are just starting to talk about it, these books make a great resource for helping your family dive into God's Word. They offer a hands-on approach to teaching Bible stories that will resonate with your whole family. Together, you'll explore these stories through games, puzzles, conversation, prayer, and easy-to-manage activities. You can spend ten minutes on a story or a whole afternoon—it's all up to you.

And you won't need a long list of supplies to get started—some crayons, a pair of scissors, add a few items you can find around your house. So find a little time, grab a handful of crayons, and create fun, meaningful family time with God.

Thanks!

Sparkhouse Family

Image Credits

Image Credits (continued)